PRODIGAL DAUGHTER
HIWOT ADILOW

This is a work of fiction. All names, characters, places, and incidents are a product of the author's imagination. Any resemblance to real events or persons, living or dead, is entirely coincidental.

Published by Akashic Books
©2019 Hiwot Adilow

ISBN: 978-1-61775-740-2

All rights reserved
Printed in China
First printing

Akashic Books
Brooklyn, New York, USA
Ballydehob, Co. Cork, Ireland
Twitter: @AkashicBooks
Facebook: AkashicBooks
E-mail: info@akashicbooks.com
Website: www.akashicbooks.com

African Poetry Book Fund
Prairie Schooner
University of Nebraska
110 Andrews Hall
Lincoln, Nebraska 68588

TABLE OF CONTENTS

PREFACE
by Mahtem Shiferraw

The daughter in Ethiopian-American poet, Hiwot Adilow's chapbook, *Prodigal Daughter*, is lustrous. Unapologetic in her wanting. She moves steadily and slowly, existing within invisible boundaries the world has set out for her. But she is also this: raw, new, filled with unrelenting passion, questioning everything that surrounds her world. Stubborn in her probing, this daughter asks questions she cannot answer, and holds herself responsible for the rebellions of her own body. This body is everything: ravaged, sentient, a home.

Hiwot Adilow, who now lives in America, says, "the only country I have is my sense / and my senses. The only language I know, / is my body and all its flinching notes" (no preponderance). She turns the body into a map of sorts, the cartography that leads the reader into a series of intricate dwellings. There, the body lives unshaken, it unfurls upon itself, gluttonous and free, defending itself from the aching of the world through small pleasures. It tasks the prodigal daughter accordingly: to be luxuriant, to give herself to a temporary pleasure ("Task of the Prodigal Daughter"), commanding her to accept its limitations, its little liberties.

> For Ages, my daughters and I were chosen by the Lord.
> We were loved and in love had the enemy underfoot.
> Sin sauntered through my walls. I became littered
> with bones, a blot on the Lord's eye, bedmate of strangers.
> ("Jerusalem Talks Back")

It is truly remarkable how the poet exerts herself onto the page in *The Prodigal Daughter*, and how quickly she turns herself to the desires of the body, which requires a finely tuned and almost surgical penwomanship. Here is a body covered with scars, inflicted by mothers, fathers, lovers, dimming traditions, and, remarkably, even by tizita. Here is a body containing many sins, and none at the same time—a body conflicted with itself, filled with beautiful contradictions. These poems are everything the body wants and needs to be: facts, lamentations, curiosities, and incessant cravings—a body filled with hunger and longing, but with knowledge too. This, perhaps, is the strongest armor the body has against the world: it knows what it wants, what it needs, and in the process of it all, it loses itself. In "Homecoming," this negotiation of the self, shifting between self-assertion and awareness and then self-denial in the face of human relationships, is one of the striking features of this collection:

> All day my mom calls me Sister and I bare my teeth to hide a wince.
> I deny the itch for whiskey, drink my water, cut the cake, thank everybody
> in the room for showing up. Licking at the bit of sugar at the bottom of
>   my little cup,
> I'm revived by the simple pleasure of my tongue's quick and private flick.
> If this were really a party of my own design there'd be wine and even
>   dancing.
> This isn't what I wanted but regardless I'm here and she's happy. I pull
>   the weeds,
> plant the flowers, pour the water, sift the dirt, dig the old lilies out by the
>   bulbs.

What is even more remarkable, perhaps, is the fact that Adilow has taken the rigorous traditions that dictate the woman's body, particularly those stemming from a clearly Ethiopian upbringing, and shaped them to her own liking. Her speaker, then, is defiant without being disrespectful; amorous and raw, dwindling in her swing between rage and inquisition, resulting in a passionate abandonment of herself to the world of small pleasures. But through it all, the speaker does not attempt to extricate herself from such rigorous traditions that demand she abide by certain rules. Rather, the poems are the hymns that command the remaking of the speaker, and through them, she is truly defined, renewed, taking upon herself the task of the prodigal daughter, saying, "I'm already slaughtered—that's a daughter. / I'm spat out, set back on fire. A bad sacrifice. Never tender enough" ("I stopped dreaming of heaven"). And on fire she is indeed. She is relentless in her wanting—she is predator and prey, daughter and mother, soft, vulnerable, but astonishingly strong in her beliefs, in her protection of a body ravaged by many things. Hers is a speaker so strong, and so attuned with the wants and needs of her body, that she gains the strength to summon the God of gods, invoking His name so she can be left in the hands of His enemy (specifically men), commanding, "let me weep bitterly! Let me burn." In the same breath, she declares that she is glad to give in to her desires: "this treachery of mine is worthwhile" ("Jerusalem Talks Back"). It's not that the speaker has succumbed to her sins, but is empowered by them, so emboldened that she finds new elements to redefine herself, and more importantly, to redefine her kind in the eyes of God.

This, in fact, is her new praise; and she grows in her glory, choosing to remember only the kind gesture from a violent ritual, refusing to be left behind, or to be left at all, relying solely on the senses of her body to guide her in the world, and to map out ways for her to exist boldly outside of herself. Though she is a quiet woman, and not made to scream about her killing ("the softest parts are black"), she is also ironclad, chasing away the devils of the world. Adilow is a new poet of great talent; she commands her poems like her speaker commands her body, picking up the limbs, choosing her killings, praying her way through things, thinking about angry fathers and hopeful mothers, offering herself as the sacrificial lamb, and throwing herself in the fire of it all—a precise and truly gifted poetess.

TIME TRAVEL THROUGH OBZ

I wrap my thighs around your solid legs and we zoom
past the mountain's edge, beyond a dog park, another lover would have left me
to walk, which I would not mind were this town less toothy and unknown to me.
Your bike brings me to my own loaned room, where I draw my small joys
from morning, where I shake off the musk of a brief night and walk
through the sun into a day that's all mine.

In a city swarmed with caves, I let electric rails rock me. I'm carried across time
and towards my own quiet, familiar bed. In truth, I walk past patch lawns
and use the glinting key that reads DEFIANT to open my mother's door and bow
my head beneath her roof. To walk into her kitchen, to feed myself what I have lost
or lent or left in the night's mouth, between the night's pursed lips incanting
my name 'til I forget where I am.

GETTING DRESSED

in ruffles and taffeta, dressed in matching sweats,
in bright fuschia socks, rocking a baldie in church

pants cut into shorts, in dress shirts tied into knots,
singing the next verse chuckling under the moon.

Jupiter and Venus cloaked beneath the peachfuzz
buds on my upper lip, the few sprouts of thick hair

grown into carpets all over my killer legs, bared
like I forgot I thought shame was a virtue. I saw

rigid postures of gossip disguised as delight split
rooms in bilateral pews, the choir swayed palm up

in pomegranate gowns, babies clapped in 2/2
time entranced by praise to dance and laugh

while mothers clocked the proverbs 31 t-shirt
my mom got to announce I'd make a good bride

someday, a rib to be equally yoked, but I shirked
glory, rent my garments, ran barking toward the erotic

slobbering like Eve in the garden starved by want;
a taste of true knowledge in what I hypothesized.

TASK OF THE PRODIGAL DAUGHTER

To be luxuriant, to give myself to a temporary pleasure,
that pressure of a thumb pressed against a bruise
consoling the blood eager to flee yet trapped.

Pinch strip soundless snap of a scab ripped
flesh now adorned with a simple jewel
too thick to dribble down the elbow or wrist
only budding against cotton or some other gentle touch
that reminds it: this is what you chose and this is where it left you,
feeble, dripping, a sea goes where the tide pulls.

I wish I could say I am more than what I was taught to be,
more than hurt rising to the surface to hum
only the chord's cry, the bed left messied,
an expanse of silence, expensive regret.

I know I don't talk to God often,
let His image straddle me instead.
It's easier to hold the thing God made
than admit or repent.

BIT TOO HARD

Took a tooth to my nipple, tore my tit from the root.
Who abandoned whom is of no consequence.

Where else can I weep as openly as this?

After the hinge ripped, he peered in uninvited,
told me what he found, scooped out a palm
of oil from my open chest, used the grease
to oil me, how else could I have kept my lips wet?

I STOPPED DREAMING OF HEAVEN

I stopped dreaming of heaven, stopped wanting to ever go home,
sat knuckle to knuckle for years, the dawn hair torn onto the altar
by my braids and made to chant. Like a mother, the Lord welts skin,
demands to be the only God. In her eyes I am always a child,
in her mouth I'm a well-oiled lamb. Onions under my collar, peppers
take the place of my tongue. I'm already slaughtered—that's a daughter.
I'm spat out, set back on fire. A bad sacrifice. Never tender enough.

NO PREPONDERANCE

I'm drawing back from invocation now.
I'm leaning in, to the myth/the heresy/the hearsay.
What was it? Whatever. What peeled me from the stage
and had me gnashing at the walls?
My tongue drips thick embers across
the floor, burns bridges and monuments.
It ribbons after me like a flag.
The only country I have is my sense
and my senses. The only language I know
is my body and all its flinching notes.

JERUSALEM TALKS BACK

So, You've forsaken me.
I was the daughter You dreamt up—
adorned in gold, singing out Your name.

Leave me here then, in the hands of Thine enemy
who swarmed up from Your sons.
My daughters and I cry and You are speechless.
You, forever living, forever needing praise.

For ages, my daughters and I were chosen by the Lord.
We were loved and in love had the enemy underfoot.
Sin sauntered through my walls. I became littered
with bones, a blot on the Lord's eye, bedmate of strangers.

Let me weep bitterly! Let me burn.
I couldn't guard myself from glutton.
I chose to devour and in devouring was made glad.
I flew into a violence like Your own jealous wrath.
Picking men limp from my mouth one by one.
I'm a thousand husbands in and wrapped with teeth.

Thine lash whipped and struck across my face.
In due time mine enemies will join me, wailing
from towers of crumbled gold while You watch
from Your seat in the clouds.

If You are merciful, If You are that God of Jacob
who wrestled an angel to earn his gifts,
this treachery of mine is worthwhile.

Let this be renamed praise: my lips thick in purple song,
exalting the small knot in my lap, sucking honey
from my knuckles, drinking wine in bed sweat-drenched
from dance my feet like small gods themselves compelled
by ravenous thirst toward a river to groan, to be born, again and again.

HOMECOMING

All day my mom calls me Sister and I bare my teeth to hide a wince.
I deny the itch for whiskey, drink my water, cut the cake, thank everybody
in the room for showing up. Licking at the bit of sugar at the bottom of my
    little cup,
I'm revived by the simple pleasure of my tongue's quick and private flick.
If this were really a party of my own design there'd be wine and even dancing.
This isn't what I wanted but regardless I'm here and she's happy. I pull the weeds,
plant the flowers, pour the water, sift the dirt, dig the old lilies out by the bulbs.

After all her labor, my mother deserves to be proud. I sit in a red dress with my
legs crossed, sweating. Coffee chars slow on the stove, she bows around the room
with smoke in her hands. I wave and claim my cup, shroud my shoulders with
blessings that I've earned and hope to keep. Tuning in and out of hymns, I listen
for my name. I count missing faces, smiling when I remember to be gracious for
the sake of everybody in the room. I keep in the lamentations but my tattoo slips.
Baldheaded, I balk, pull my arm back. I stay in, come home before night. I pray
when asked to pray and grow my glory. I can't change the way I walk but I try
to pay attention. So many promises I can't keep. I hold steadfast to secrets.
I smile and stand beside her like a little crooked mirror.

TIZITA

Shawled in white and lined in gold, Tizita looks behind her and waves as the
    plane ascends.
She never says goodbye. She's always close. She wakes up yesterday. It's a new place.
She stands for years, quietly stirring a pot, with the window open, watching the
    snow.
The smell of shiro, shinquirt, gomen soaks into her hair and clothes.

I eat with my right hand and feed my mother what I won't swallow. The hard yolk,
her favorite part. I wash my hands all day and am still afraid to touch my face,
    to burn
my eyes. My chest's on fire and my shirt is stained. I eat too fast, let the neighbor
    kiss
my face. She says I'm like a kid from back home and my mother purrs and draws
    me close.

EXORCISM

The bishop who first held her underwater (in Jesus name)
catches her as she's tossed toward the altar, in Jesus name.

Four fingers pressed hard against her damp forehead, eyes
clamped, she prays now for prayer to end. In Jesus name,

she's touched again by a swarm; the laying on of hands
demands her many spirits die quick. *Leave her, in Jesus name!*

Splayed against the hums she heaves, grateful for at least
the cover of unending noise, the freedom to weep, in Jesus name!

While you cry, Hiwot, recall her hand on the small of your back,
being tangled in bed while she prayed for you, in Jesus name.

WALATTA PETROS PRAYS ABOUT DESIRE

I still don't know what it means
to unfurl, like a kiss across her arms.
My faith is a tongue shoveled into Your ear.
Lord, do you hear me?

WIVES AND LOVERS

We may very well succumb to our cowardice.
Likely, we'll become the women our mothers
dreamt up when we bit their nipples and pulled
for what would make us full.

Childless, I wonder—with a man's knuckles
spanning my lap—about a life spent like this,
forever with his tenor and bass calling me to sing.
The work of sugar always put on me.

I think of another honey-lipped woman crooning
to her man, his skin the color of praline and semi-sweet.
What's tender in the notes, soft and thrumming, comes from me.
Rises near her trilling tongue; saves the bite for what we barely knew.

The bite is always what we won't know, what a quiet life
comes up with. A hit against our teeth.

AFTER THE DINNER PARTY

She's standing, open handed, with her head down, collecting plates.
Heineken trickles through her still-black tresses and the bubbles smudge
the smile off her face. She stares at the green glass bottles on the table.
They match the green of the couch where the guests sit.

Their eyes catch the yellow light that drips.
Their eyes throw light to the floor like dust.
When they go, they shake her hand and nod
as if to say *we won't tell anyone what we've seen*

tonight. She moves to the kitchen, a pan in her hand.
Her husband comes behind her, smiles his rare smile.
He pulls her body close to his as if she were another
of his limbs. She flinches and wields the pan like a knife.

CA·COPH'O·NOUS

(kəˈkäfənəs) [[prob. via Fr *cacophonie* < ML *cacophonia* < Gr kakophōnía < kakophōnos, harsh sounding < *kakos*, bad evil + phōnḗ, voice: see PHONO-]] **adj. 1.** *harsh sounding*: as in, the *cacophonous* cat trapped scratching behind the wall esp. as it chases a smaller creature it might eat; two beasts churning through plaster is a *cacophonous* announcement of predator and prey. **2.** *noisy*: busted lip shot cool with ice; phones ring in every room; whistle bell alarm buzz pull of the day's beginning and end; a room with the TV blaring and the lights shut off; the hall as I feared she might fall down the steps; the dial tone; the siren; a sobbing child refusing sides; a fight where blood is drawn and teeth are lost; rapturous laughter; the laying on of hands and its aftermath **3.** *discordant*: an argument in a language you half know and don't speak; being told to leave and begged to come back home; a body thrown against the blacks and whites; the triad of diminished chords held air tight; crashingcrashingcrashing strikes

MY FATHER WON'T FORGIVE ME

I'm the only one who wasn't hit,
    who dialed and ushered butchers to the door.
Before the phone rings, my mother sleeps
    in my bed. I turn to wake with her nestled
for balm against my small back.

My brother's on the floor, his own dimpled hand
    holding where our father slapped.
This isn't why he cries. It's the sight of our dad
    shrunken and cuffed, the hard seat
in the precinct while we wait.

STORE FRONT PROJECT, 1964

After Christo and Jeanne-Claude

I feel unwelcome in public
spaces and walk with my face
in my phone trying to find a
song that might make this
afternoon more pleasant keep
me from feeling followed or
otherwise awkward as I move
through the great white halls
where the African art is tucked
in the shadowy back, I bet they
mean nothing by this I can't
help but notice I'm stopped by
a series of pieces that look like a
city being planned this corner
draped like an abandoned
painting a map of fraught lines
those empty storefronts like a
hot ass August against the
black cool downstairs bar
where beer is poured and jazz
is played and gin is drunk a city
proud to sell dreams of liberty
and debt, small drawn
storefronts like the ones on
Columbia Ave where Odessa's
car stalled and she was
manhandled like an animal by
the cops what gets built in a

city what gets left what gets
bought who to watch in a city
marked up at the margins who
gets robbed who has to move
who gets left to rot

THE SOFTEST PARTS ARE BLACK

After Jay Katelansky

I'm a quiet woman. I'm not made to scream about my killing or my made-dead.

I'm not made to scream unless I'm laughing at a joke. I laugh with my whole body

and all my skin. When I weep (because the world ain't always how I'd have it

and won't ever have me like I'd like) I pave my throat with ice. I edge my lips

with barb. I speak in secret code and hope the haters keep at bay.

They peep and mechanize and all my armor melts and rusts.

(The things I wore for war were bound to wear.

Imported, extorted, and turned into my name,

I only use these tools to play their game.)

I'm a velvet lady by birth.

I'm a honeydip.

I'm dipped in silk.

I deserve my peace.

I've got promises to keep:

I'm not here to spend my garden on the graves my haters made.

I came to give flowers to my friends while we're alive.

I came to plant trees, for fruit. A jacaranda that spills purple

in spring. I want to kiss my friends on the face and leave

lipstick on all their chiseled cheeks.

If I could have my wish, I wouldn't have to watch

my softest parts turn to stone. Wouldn't need a

a bullet or a gun. Everybody's texting to say *stay alive.*

I don't want to be a liar. If I could have my wish,

I'd keep my promises. Flowers would pool around us

and we'd dance in the garden I tilled with my two hands.

IRONCLAD, I CHASED AWAY THE DEVIL

I'm gonna put on a iron shirt, and chase Satan out of earth.

—*Max Romeo*

Ironclad, I chased away the devil. I sent him to the sun to burn.
Every corner of the world is a warm bed where you sleep sound.
No waterlogged lungs. No running from gunfire to more fire.
No oil-sick earth. No poison-spiked seas or drinking water.
No war for oil. No land bordered by cartographers
who see Europe as the sun and everyone spinning
around it like it's God. No gods with blue eyes.
No gods with white hair and white skin. No kin-fucking kings
of the confederacy as gods of parliament. No parliament
unless it brings us Funk. No fucking men who can't take no.
No dead sisters of any body. No bombed houses of God.
No bombs dropped on children, asleep or awake or at all.
In the afterward is a world built on this message: everyone
stays alive until they die a sweet and quiet death of ancient age.
The only noise made is the sound of skin on skin, the puckerflick of a kiss.

ACKNOWLEDGMENTS

The following poems have appeared in these publications:

"the softest parts are black" first appeared in *WusGood? Magazine*
"no preponderance" first appeared in *Vinyl*
"Wives and Lovers" first appeared online at the Brunel International African
Poetry Prize site